InSpiration-A Day At A Time

I0159477

By Miranda Carey-Jones

About the Author

Miranda Carey-Jones is a psychotherapist, life coach, magnet therapist, reiki master and nutritionist, qualified and certified by the AADP – American Association of Drugless Practitioners.

An ex international event rider from Great Britain has had many reasons to use the affirmations that appear in this book...sports psychology being one of the big things when competing at a high level, to keep your head, don't let things get to you and NEVER GIVE UP.

Moved to USA from Europe, where she had a successful competition yard full of event horses and an equine therapy centre.

CEO of Personal Care Products Company - Spa health LLC

www.spahealth.co

Also available from MC Publishing -Toxic by Miranda Carey-Jones

Dedication and Inspiration/Thanks

I owe this to my parents for their continuous support in every aspect of my life, their kindness, their positive minds, their intelligent outlook on life. They inspire me and encourage every venture that I take part in. Thank you Mum and Dad ...Peter and Pamela Carey.

To my daughter Ally, who constantly inspires me with her incredible mind, enthusiasm , interest and love of life.

Also to my "kick in the pants" partner, Mark Hightower, when the going gets rough , the tough get going... He has always been there for me , and the going was tough at times...but constant encouragement and gentle nudges kept my road onward bound.. Thank you Mark.

And to my Grandmother, who has encouraged me in so many ways , backing my wild ventures ...thank you Guggy- June MacDonald

To my wonderful supportive Aunt , Giddy- Virginia Cottrell, who has always been there for me, helping whenever needed.

Thanks to all my family who have been so great. Each and every one of you have been such an inspiration, in so many different ways.

Huge thanks to Molly Perry for the illustrations.

Thank you all.

Foreword:-

This book inspires you one day at a time to create your own pathway in life. To give you positive thoughts and ideas to live life to the fullest in the happiest way, understanding why. ' Cause life is weird...we don't always understand what's in store for us.

Each day of the month has a different quotation/meaning/lesson to help you through difficult and testing times, or to just remind you of how you should be thinking. You can be fit physically and mentally too, you can attract anything that you wish for, unleash the power from within...

Use the chapters as meditation or for positive thoughts throughout the day. Change your thought pattern to suit your individual needs, be full of joy and happiness.

There are many prophecies of how things are, will be and could be. This is the simplest way to create and achieve maximum abundance within your life and to help make the world a nicer, better place...follow instructions to the last t...

Introduction:-

You have the Power-You are the Power...

Warning :- Power is Toxic- Use wisely..

Everyone goes through a transitional period in their lives, for various reasons, this book teaches you how to deal with these periods.

Like winning at sports, losing weight, being successful at your job – all take effort, mind over matter...

This book is to create inspiration amongst those who feel lost, need guidance, to show them another way . If this doesn't apply to you at the time, it may, if shared , help a friend or family member in need- a lot of people keep things bottled up inside., not knowing how to deal with their problems.

How to better yourself and understand why things happen, in a few easy steps.

Everything happens for a Reason

Put yourself into top gear and see fantastic personal results , that result in all round achievement ...

BE AN INSPIRATION- LEAVE A LEGACY- be an icon, a hero to someone, to your children, those around you, show kindness, don't be afraid to speak out.

Chapters 1 -30

Chapter 1

Focus

Everything Is meant to be....your path is already drawn out for you, you may divert from this path every once in a while but you always get rerouted back to it...Mistakes...you have to make them to be who you are, you have to learn...we are not born with this wisdom that we can be so complacent to think we are better than any living thing...we have to LEARN...

What do you want from your life....Focus on what you truly want.... Do not focus on what you don't want, or you will get that...FOCUS on good things and abundance...

Be grateful for every experience, good or bad, as they made you who you are today.

Chapter 2

The Law of Attraction

Get rid of negativity….even if someone is being nasty to you, to your face or behind your back. Send back love to this person…

Like attracts Like…if you send bad thoughts and anger back…or even think them…you are your thoughts…these things will stay with you and come back on you daily…say thank you to the nasty person for they have made you who you are today…a much stronger wiser person… Say what you really mean, what you really want, not say things to please anyone, it will end in tears if you say you like something you don't really like, just to fit in…Be you…

Without "communication", there is no relationship.

Without "respect", there is no love.

Without "trust , there is no hope.

Look out for these 3 powerful words and use them wisely.

Chapter 3

Protection

Listen to guidance, look for signs, trust your gut feeling, listen to your heart...who or what is yours? Practice this and see that you are never alone, you are always being guided by your loved ones in spirit.. NEVER GIVE UP

Focus on an intention – your mind and body will follow suit.

If you want something enough you will get it, be careful of what you do ask for , as you could get it!!!

Be selective about who you socialize with...negative people are venomous...lethal for your productive path forwards...cleanse your life of these people and situations that cause toxicity.

Break Free from the chains (thoughts and beliefs) that bind you....

Accomplish your goals, do what you set out to do.

Chapter 4

Ego

The Ego- not to be confused with self confidence (which is a powerful belief)....this is a big thing that most of us have problems with.....ME ME ME...boost oneself up!!!

You must do things because you want to do things, not because you feel , what could I get from this situation...if you genuinely give from your heart something that you love and cherish too then that will come back on you 10 fold..

Try not to put people down, especially in front of others... to boost your ego, do you feel good from this?

Cockiness is often little more than a camouflage for self- doubt- ask yourself what insecurities are you compensating for by pumping up your ego.

Food for thought!!!

Don't boast- let people admire you for your talents and tell you , not the other way around..be a listener not a talker..

Try getting your energy from other sources, like nature, the sea, lakes, mountain tops, sport, meditation….try not to use/take people's energy to get what you want(however easily given)…it may work sometimes but it is a bad energy you are creating…...when you gain your own energy you feel elated, relaxed, happy and satisfied all in one…full of life, associated with mother nature and earth..spiritual…closer to God..

How many times have you gone into a room and someone isn't well…I've got this really bad illness and oh no….poor me…what happens, everyone gives their attention and energy to this person , this person leave feeling much better and everyone else feels drained

When someone makes you feel small….intimidates you in front of others or just to make themselves feel good…they leave feeling good and you feel awful and drained..

Sometimes you just don't want to be a part of something…how many times do people come and ask you what's up, what are you doing? Do you want something to drink? Etc etc….another way of gaining energy the wrong way.. you feel great having people surrounding you giving their energies…they feel drained.

Chapter 5

Creating emotions

Emotions create good or bad energy

When you surround yourself with good energy , great things happen, knock on effect...it is amazing...good thoughts bring great happenings..When you have bad energy around you, things just go wrong, just can't seem to stop the silly annoying things happening, you trip over, have your 3 bad luck things in a day, type of energy...by using the good energies below and not using the bad energy you can turn your life around to being totally positive and see results immediately... but you cannot doubt...a doubt cancels out the order you have just made subconsciously or consciously to the universe...any slight negative thought, like ok I'll order this but I'm not sure...STOP...that cancels the order...you have to wholeheartedly believe , have faith in what you want and ask for it...

Negative emotions are jealousy, regret, anger, doubt, fear, panic, dread, rage, disgust, sorrow, boredom, frustration, lying, sarcasm, selfishness.

Positive emotions are happiness, joy, laughing, smiling, singing, feeling satisfied, pleasure, desire, admiration, gratitude , thankfulness, triumph, amusement, hope, peacefulness, LOVE, kindness

Gratitude is a very powerful emotion . When you are grateful, the universe rewards you with more things to be grateful for.

FEAR stands for False Expectations Appearing Real….hasn't happened yet, this is a wasted emotion.

You must train and adapt your lifestyle to include these positive emotions.

Re-organize…reprogram your mind to different ways of thinking… with practice, it becomes easier and easier…

 Give yourself little goals each day , practice until you have them perfect.

Don't say negative things, your words and even thoughts are what you become….for example…I can't do this because I might hurt myself, the next things you know, you have manifested a trip to hospital with a cast on your limb…

You can do anything you want with this power. Next time you are slowed down or rerouted, say thank you to your guides/angels. Maybe you lost something in order to make you find something else important to you. Re-routing opportunities.

Chapter 6

Synchronicity

Fate, Destiny or Synchronicity , called by different names but lead to a positive change.

When you are going the right way/doing the right thing, everything unfolds in front of you, yay, this is the way to go...but when you find obstacles there is something telling you NOT THIS WAY...

Blessings in disguise. Saving you from a potential situation. Never push providence. Be patient and all will come to you.

Chapter 7

Everything is possible

No matter where you want to go, what you want to be, how you want to be, see yourself as just that, what it is that you want, NOT what you don't want to be...visualize, see in your mind's eye exactly who you are...and you will be it....whether it's weight loss you want, a trimmer body, more success at work, a new job, a new car, more money...EVERYTHING is possible....change your thought pattern and believe..use positive energies and words..think these 100% ....totally believe...

You have the POWER, you and only you can change your thoughts and do this...Nothing will change if nothing changes!!! Sick and tired of being sick and tired?? Then DO IT...you can!!!

Lead by example, others will follow your success..become an ICON...a HERO....that people look up to...sometimes we outgrow people on our paths and diverse, we go different directions...rest assured they will look up to you when you are using these methods to better yourself...and probably saying, well he got lucky....yes, I read this book , used my mind to make me stronger, to be able to have the power to do anything I want to do in this world...but as we digress in our relationships we find new people to accompany us on our paths, each encounter is important to us in some way to help us advance, whether short or long term, we all meet for a reason...

Self control...manipulation....everyone has a right to their own thoughts...you exercise self control by not listening to others and completing your own task...but remember you must not manipulate others into doing this, lead by example and show them what you can do.. you will lose energy by trying to make things happen for them...your HARD EARNED ENERGY!!

DO not give it away freely....

Do not play God, only God decides things...

Chapter 8

Grief

Grieving and Loss of a loved one /pet

Grieving...Unfortunately for us, not for them, but we have to let go...God has other plans for them, so we have to release, we are grieving for ourselves not for them...they were needed and are happy and free now...look for signs that they are with you and guiding you...

We enjoyed and adored their company and love here on the earth plane. We have to let go and release for them to continue on their own journey , to meet up one day with us when we have different jobs to do too...only god decides which our journey is and when our time is up, and for what reason..We, still living, have to come to terms with this loss, knowing they are still around us, by the signs left and be comforted by the fact that they are safe and helping us do our job now.

We all have a job to do here on the earth's plane, some more spiritual than others, some more glamorous than others, but each on its own so important to the universal force..and to complete the makeup of the path..

Guardian Angels are there in many different forms and guises to support you and your loved ones...when you feel a nudge in a direction or a brush of something against you, know that your guardian angel is with you...sent from Heaven above to guide you, be comforted by this and know you are loved and looked after..

Chapter 9

Losing a job

Maybe you have manifested this? Maybe subconsciously you disliked what you were doing? So you put out a request for this to change..or maybe you asked for something better, when one door closes another opens..the universe will ALWAYS provide...

When one door closes , another opens. Maybe not as quickly as you hoped for but there will be a lesson in there too...what did you ask for? Were you very specific? If you were, expect a miracle, for the better job, a huge offer...you will always get the sum total of what you deserve.

Think about it, do you deserve a great job with full perks? If you have always done things right in your life then you will be rewarded...if not you will have some more lessons to learn from and then success will follow...

Chapter 10

Where do signs come from?

A feather, number sequences, music, repeated sightings, of removal vans -maybe you are going to move in the near future, clocks and watches stopping..telling you that you need to restart your life again...big changes happen like that..some people are visual whereas others hear things, feel things..each person is different and interprets the sign in a different way..

If you see 11-11- or sequences similar , on a clock, digital or computer, a road number – choose your thoughts carefully, think of things you truly want and not what you don't want. An opportunity is in the offing.

When things appear when you want an answer.

Chapter 11

Feel the high

Achievement is a high...feel the feeling...success is a high...

When things don't feel right and aren't going your way, think what have your thoughts been doing, how did you word your last sarcastic comment, trying to impress someone? It all comes back on you...even in jest, you still thought it and said it...

How to reverse the wrong? Say in your mind- please rewind what I just said/thought, and replace it with a positive thought immediately to counteract your negative thought.

Personal Goals...achieve the best you can possibly achieve, discover your hidden talents, feel proud of yourself, feel the achievement...

Without these 4 words in your life you have nothing – Love, Honesty, Truth and Respect.

Chapter 12

Aggression

Aggressive behavior attracts more aggressive behavior...more about the Ego...world wars wouldn't happen if they loved each other, it's toxic hate and craving POWER, instead of seeking it in spiritual ways...feeding the aggressor's ego...I control, I can and I have the power...watch me...a dangerous combination that will get ousted after a while..

Dictatorship !!!

Chapter 13

Timing

Universal timing...Everything happens in your life at precisely the right time and for the right reason- even if you don't agree with it- they know better...whether good or bad energy, it has come to you when you most need it to learn something or experience something important for your path.

If your gut doesn't feel good doing something, DON'T DO IT- follow your gut feeling always..

Chapter 14

Animals and thoughts

We should look more at animals and how they behave...they inspire us, never complain, give unconditional love, protect with all their heart...give comfort when needed..and they pick up on bad energy a mile off and warn you...amazing creatures of God..

Often wondered why animals choose who they like and who they don't..? They read your thoughts...yep... it's true...they can see through the outer niceness and under the façade...to the nasty thoughts, either nasty about the dog or nasty about its owner and situation/surroundings..Be careful what you think or you'll lose a trouser leg!!!

Be Realistic -Expect a Miracle

Chapter 15

Achievement

Achieve/Optimism versus pessimism/accomplishment

Be the best that you can possibly be, give your all and it will be enough...try your hardest at anything/everything you do/want and you will achieve...NEVER GIVE UP...

When you feel a negative thought, start doing something to occupy your mind and change your thought pattern.

Don't forget that you inspire others' too, from your own actions, show them what you can do, what you are made of, people copy success, feel the success, BE an Inspiration...

People will look up to you and follow you, stand tall Be confident, attract goodness.

"I CAN'T" doesn't exist... they are negative words...there is always a CAN somewhere if you look for it...

Mind over Matter

Chapter 16

Seeking Attention

How many people you know do things for attention, from shouting out loudly above other people, to interrupting , to endangering their lives, or someone else's..so often happens..if you attracted attention the good way you wouldn't need to behave in a strange weird manner to become "noticed", you would be anyway....you don't need to "stand out" -you already would...tattoos, rasta hair, body piercings, bright colours, crime, all unnecessary, to whom are you making the statement...YOURSELF, no-one else...no-one else cares...if this makes you happy then great, you are doing it for the right reason.

Compliment people, be kind..never take advantage of kindness, weakness or ignorance...

When we want/crave attention, we sometimes become ill...this attracts a poor me attitude/attention, but was this the real attention that you subconsciously wanted and asked for?

Chapter 17

How to make change happen

Behavioural Pattern- if you want change, you have to change your thoughts and actions.

Appreciation and Respect has to be earned , and is gained by giving it... having values, morals and high principles will attract success and abundance into your life..

It's all a mirror, reflecting yourself- your good and bad thoughts...

If you don't "get it" , you repeat until you do...

To reverse the negative thought, say I'm sorry, please forgive me, I'm so grateful for (all the great things in your life, list them) and then say a big thank you to the divine, feel grateful, and feel abundance flow through you .. hold that feeling...remember what it feels like...ask it into your day many times during the day...create abundance in your life for good...only takes a bit of practice..

Every good thing you do comes back 10 fold...same with bad things...watch out!!!

Don't procrastinate- DO IT NOW!!!

Keep positive people by your side...those who encourage you and thrive on your success and goal getting.

Chapter 18

Where do bad energies come from?

Newspapers, negative people, negative situations, something you read, television, movies especially, bad negative emotions that people relate to in their lives and thrive on the poor me and aggressor syndrome...psychotic behavior arrives from these sources, let's try it and see what happens, adding to more worldly crime, addiction and aggression... also comes from having a "need"...a need is negative, change that to a "want" and you will receive...

Jealousy creates a lot of nasty thoughts and actions too..look inwards to keep these thoughts at bay, they only harm the person who thinks them...

Sarcasm- the lowest form of wit....yet people use it to boost their egos daily, to make themselves feel good...without realizing its detrimental force against them and their order of universal wants.

If you fill your life with drama and sadness, the more you will invite.

Chapter 19

How long does this take to happen?

The Divine Universal energy is constantly giving and receiving, but your limiting belief system is stopping them coming through…Train your thoughts to allow your belief system to constantly receive and you will…things will just happen…amazing …try it!!

Love to Love- it attracts all good!!!

Recite as many times a day as you feel the need to… "I have unlimited abundance" , feel the joy whilst receiving it…this covers EVERYTHING…health, wealth, happiness, love, luck…

Chapter 20

Self Esteem

Forgive your mistakes, these too shall pass..

We cannot live amongst the same for long, when you are down on the wheel of life the only way is up..

Today is the 1st day of my life... repeat this along with good vibes like I love you, thank you...

CARPE DIEM- seize the day!!!

Boost yourself by your achievements. Not looking for egoism. Nor credit, but credit where credit is due.

Beauty is in the eye of the beholder, we see and are what we want to see and be. You are beauty.

When I look back on all these worries I remember the story of the old man who said on his deathbed that he had had a lot of trouble in his life, MOST of which NEVER happened!!!!

#Winston Churchill#

Chapter 21

But it's not happening-HELP???

When things go wrong, look at what you "expected " to happen/be...

Do you, even though, you have manifested for good things to happen and been adamant about it, have you maybe felt you didn't "deserve" it, or didn't really "expect" it to happen??

Thereby you attracted the negative emotion of not deserving into your life...The universe immediately cancelled the order/blocking your thoughts and gave what you really wanted...

It's no good just saying it, you must feel it within your heart and soul to receive it.

It can only work when the conscious mind and subconscious minds believe and have faith, are at one...

When things go wrong we look to blame something, someone, anything will do , to put the onus onto somebody else, to relieve the feeling of helplessness/uselessness/guilt.

Don't look for faults, look for a cure.

Do you give credit for your achievements to the same as you blame for your failures?

Accept responsibilities for your own actions

Don't be a victim!!!

When in deep water , paddle faster

Chapter 22

Forgiveness

Forgiveness is a powerful emotion, you may not forget but to forgive releases you of negativity that was struggling to burst out, stopping you from completing your order, allowing abundance to flow through your now pure thoughts.

If it wasn't for the mistakes of the people and the hurt they caused you, you wouldn't have been able to achieve so much and be you. They made you who you are, be grateful...

Problems are only opportunities in work clothes!!!

If the world , one by one, started to think good thoughts and send love to all there would be no need for adversity and war, hate would disappear in the shadow of love..

Chapter 23

Imperfection

Accept imperfection- see how well you have done, what you have achieved...be grateful for what you can do... and how you are.

We are learning all our lives, so how can we be PERFECT? Try to be the best that we can, don't put too much emphasis on the result.... enjoy the journey.

To everyone you meet and talk to, be happy , talk about good things, not "impending" doom as people love to express whilst knowing more than others...GOSSIP!!! Look for the good in everyone....see the good in everyone...it's there...you might just have to have an opportunity to bring it out.

Relationships- destructive relationships come from negative feelings being suppressed.

 No-one loves the man he fears.

Accept others' imperfections , do not try and change them. If they want to change they will do so of their own accord, if not , leave well alone.

Be careful how you use your tone of voice, this may be misconstrued as negativity, sarcasm or anger.

Chapter 24

Methods to initiate good thoughts and moods

Use these simple techniques to create the moods to make you feel great.

1) Soft music
2) Candles – create an atmosphere/mood
3) Burn Essential oils
4) Go for a walk, commune with nature
5) Meditate
6) Climb a mountain, the summit will create enormous amounts of abundant energy
7) Be by the sea, the ebb and flow of the tide will cleanse your emotions leaving you feeling refreshed and renewed mentally and physically
8) Play an instrument
9) Play with animals or children, cuddle them, release the feel good factor
10) Sing or dance creates very good energy
11) Massage
12) Read a book

Chapter 25

Disappointment

Know that you have to feel this emotion in order to go forwards with a big determined leap...someone or thing/situation may have let you down , in your opinion, but is only rerouting you to bigger stuff...all a part of the path you are taking... Keep on keeping on , smile and face the world happy, attract more joy.

When we blame ourselves or others, we create a block.

Let go, release – live for the now- walk through the door.

Don't sweat the small stuff

Ask and it shall be given, seek and you shall find.

Chapter 26

Enthusiasm is contagious... Have fun, play like a child...forget the real world and enter the world through a child's eyes, smile , laugh and enjoy!!!

Challenge is good....disconnect and follow your dreams...Honesty and integrity...takes a bigger man to say I'm sorry...

Make someone feel special, remember that all these feelings come back on you...these lovely warm snuggly feelings...

Sometimes you face a difficulty/problem not because you are doing something wrong but maybe you are doing something right...altering your path..go with the flow.

Chapter 27

Respect

Be respectful, say please and thank you, it goes a long way, you will get respect back from it.

Let go, stop holding grudges...it's holding you back...abide by the rules of the universal law...

Never judge someone, you don't know what they are going through in their own world.

If you are not doing something you enjoy , stop wasting your time and do something that inspires you, never too late to change your path.

When you are down on the wheel of life, the only way is up, the wheel turns continuously.

Treat others as you wish to be treated yourself.

Be a reflection of what you want to see in others.

Be honest and you will receive honesty.

Be loving and you will receive love.

Be kind and you will receive kindness.

Give and you will receive.

Chapter 28

Attitude

Good and Bad attitude

Accept that not everyone has a good attitude towards you and life...try to change your own attitude into a positive one, great outlook on life with gracious feelings... you will reap the harvest from this work...

Bad attitude gets people into bad situations, jail/court/ inviting speeding fines and "bad luck"...call it bad luck or call it karma from the universe...you can change that right now...be positive and say you're sorry, I love you, and thank you for all the good in my life...

DO NOT focus on the bad...forget it. leave it behind!!!

Chapter 29

Don't waste your chances

God and the universe give you many chances to do right- not to waste (food, electricity), teaching you things are valuable, not to lie....not to cheat or steal, not to commit adultery, not to be a glutton...

If you continue to make the same mistakes you will be stopped and have to repeat the lesson over and over until you get it right.

Teach your kids and young folk around you values from the start, they will grow up having respect for things that have to be worked for, for things that are given.

 Knowing of the poor people around the world who have nothing, whatever the young of today have , it is more than they have.

Things you have to give up in order to get something else.

Chapter 30

You make the decisions, only you... to get where you want to, no one else can choose...it's your life, grab the reins and - GO GO GO.

Good things come to those that are strong, dedicated and motivated...be organized, de- clutter your closet, de-clutter your life....tidy mind, tidy life...

Detox your whole mind, body and soul. You are your thoughts, your diet, your life...

Stick to your word, if you say you will do something, regardless of what comes up, keep your word...do not disappoint people...don't look for credit in saying you will do things and then let them down by not turning up or forgetting/not wanting to do it...

Endless possibilities and opportunities open up for you when you practice these few lessons.

Conclusion

I hope you like this book and use it to obtain the best possible outcome, I hope you change your lives around and remember the words...it helped me to write it, so I thank you for now reading it.

With each new day we are given new hope, new possibilities, new opportunities.

Seize the opportunities.

Each new day is a miracle.

www.ingramcontent.com/pod-product-compliance
Lightning Source LLC
Chambersburg PA
CBHW060634030426
42337CB00018B/3359